Structural Wonders

Machu Picchu

Gillian Richardson

Published by Weigl Publishers Inc.
350 5th Avenue, Suite 3304, PMB 6G
New York, NY 10118-0069

Website: www.weigl.com

Library of Congress Cataloging-in-Publication Data

Richardson, Gillian.
 Machu Picchu / Gillian Richardson.
    p.cm. – (Structural wonders)
 Includes index.
 ISBN 978-1-59036-943-2 (soft cover: alk. Paper)—
 ISBN 978-1-59036-942-5 (hard cover: alk. Paper)
1. Machu Picchu Site (Peru)—Juvenile literature.
2. Inca architecture—Juvenile literature.
3. Peru—Antiquities—Juvenile literature. I. title.
F3429.1.M3R53 2009
985'.37—dc22

2008015666

Printed in the United States of America
1 2 3 4 5 6 7 8 9 0 12 11 10 09 08

Photograph Credits

Weigl would like to acknowledge Getty Images as one of its primary image suppliers
for this book.

Every reasonable effort has been made to trace ownership and to obtain
permission to reprint copyright material. The publishers would be pleased
to have any errors or omissions brought to their attention so that they may
be corrected in subsequent printings.

All of the internet URLs given in the book were valid at the time of publication.
However, due to the dynamic nature of the Internet, some addresses may have
changed, or sites may have ceased to exist since publication. While the author
and publisher regret any inconvenience this may cause readers, no responsibility
for any such changes can be accepted by either the author or the publisher.

Project Coordinators: Heather C. Hudak, Heather Kissock
Design: Terry Paulhus

Contents

What is Machu Picchu?

Some of the most exciting **archaeological** finds include the remains of human structures built long ago. In remote places, such as forests, the discovery of these remains is often unexpected. They lead to new knowledge about the ancient cultures and civilizations that built them. Machu Picchu is such a place.

Machu Picchu is located about 70 miles (112 kilometers) from Cuzco, the center of the ancient Inca Empire. It sits at the top of a ridge between two mountain peaks at an elevation of 8,040 feet (2,451 meters), invisible from the forest and winding Urubamba River gorge below. The city's stone-walled buildings and **terraced** fields cover about 5 square miles (13 square km).

Hidden by thick forest plants high in the Andes Mountains of Peru, South America, the Inca city lay abandoned for nearly 400 years. It was not until 1911 that the area became active again. At this time, Hiram Bingham, an assistant professor from Yale University, came upon the city's ruins.

When the overgrown forest was cut back, a community of 150 to 200 buildings was revealed. It included sacred temples and an **irrigated** farming area for growing food crops. At its peak, about 1,000 people likely lived and worked in the city.

Quick Bites
- Machu Picchu means "old mountain peak."
- A local farmer led Hiram Bingham to the ruins of Machu Picchu. He had been searching for another major city known as Vilcabamba. In 1911, Bingham found Vilcabamba deep in the forest west of Cuzco.

Building History

Machu Picchu is often called the "Lost City of the Inca." The Inca were a small tribe that lived around Cuzco in the 13th century. From 1438 to 1471, Pachacuti was the Inca ruler.

Machu Picchu is believed to have been built by Pachacuti from 1460 to 1470. When Pachacuti first started building it, Machu Picchu was meant to be part royal estate and part religious **retreat**. It would house the emperor, as well as his family, spiritual and political advisors, and servants.

Machu Picchu was one of the many construction projects built during Pachacuti's reign. The ruins of this city are an example of the architectural and engineering skills of the ancient Inca people. Besides houses, the Inca built temples for worship and used a natural spring that was thought to be sacred as a source of clean water. A **gravity**-fed system ran through stone channels to irrigate the crops that were farmed on the terraced fields.

A statue of Pachacuti stands in a town near Machu Picchu.

Since the Inca had no system of writing, there are no records, such as blueprints, to show how they planned the project. However, as archaeologists studied the site, they found that parts of Machu Picchu were reserved for specific groups and certain activities.

Thousands of miles of stone roads lead to Machu Picchu.

TIMELINE OF CONSTRUCTION

1438 to 1471: Pachacuti becomes emperor. He begins construction on several buildings and roads.

1460 to 1470: Pachacuti builds Machu Picchu as a royal estate and religious retreat.

Early 1500s: Machu Picchu is abandoned when the Spanish invade the area.

1911: American professor Hiram Bingham finds the ruins of Machu Picchu.

1981: Peru declares Machu Picchu and its surrounding area a historical sanctuary.

1983: Machu Picchu is designated a **UNESCO World Heritage Site**.

2007: Machu Picchu is named one of the New Seven Wonders of the World.

Channels that were 5 inches (12 cm) wide carried water from natural springs through fountains to the agricultural terraces.

The Intihuatana Stone is a single piece of rock 6 feet (1.8 m) tall, sculpted into a 4-sided pillar.

The site was divided into two parts—the agricultural sector and the urban sector. Crops could not grow on the steep slopes of the mountains. For this reason, the agricultural sector was located on the terraces in front of the buildings. Here, crops were grown to feed the people living at Machu Picchu. The urban sector contained the buildings of Machu Picchu. This sector itself was divided further. The north section was used for religious purposes and contained temples and other religious structures. The south contained houses and workshops. This is where laborers and military staff worked and lived. The final section of the urban sector housed the emperor and other nobility. The royal **mausoleum** was found here.

It has been discovered that 60 percent of the ruins are below ground level.

Big Ideas

Religion played an important role in the lives of the Inca. In Inca culture, religion was closely tied to nature. The people worshiped gods of the Sun, the Moon, Earth, and water. They thought of natural features, such as high mountains, underground springs, and even large stones, as sacred places. Religious rituals were held in special temples to win the favor of the gods.

The Inca were skilled at planning structures to take advantage of sacred natural features. Pachacuti likely chose the remote site of Machu Picchu because it has a view of the mountains in all directions. The closest peak, Huayna Picchu, stands like a **sentinel** to the northwest. On three sides, Machu Picchu's ridge overlooks the Urubamba River as it winds through the canyon below.

The religious theme continues inside Machu Picchu's walls. Buildings within the city include religious shrines, temples, and a royal tomb. The round Temple of the Sun is believed to have been used as a solar **observatory**. It houses a window through which the rising Sun enters on the June 21 **solstice**. Another sacred structure, the Intihuatana Stone, was used as a calendar. This 6-foot, 4-sided tapered tower acted as a **sundial** to determine midday on the exact date of the spring and fall **equinox**. On March 21 and September 21, the Sun is directly over the tower, so it casts no shadow. The Inca believed they could capture the power of the Sun at this special time. They wanted to keep the Sun from moving away and leaving them in total darkness.

1) The Urubamba River may have provided water for the Inca.
2) To the Inca, Machu Picchu's royal estate symbolized the emperor's face. Huayna Picchu was his nose. From this angle, it appears as if the emperor is looking towards the gods. 3) All of Machu Picchu can be seen from Huayna Picchu's peak.

Profile:
The Inca and Pachacuti

Inca society consisted of a ruler who was part of a royal family, nobles and priests, and common people. Their influence remained limited until around 1438 A.D., when another group of people from the north attacked Cuzco. The Inca king, Wiracocha, fled, leaving his son Yupanqui to fight the enemy. Yupanqui won this battle. He changed his name to *Pachacuti*, which means "the one who rules everything," and began to extend his control within the country now known as Peru.

From 1438 to 1471, with Pachacuti as ruler, Inca power continued to grow. By the late 1400s, he ruled an empire of about 10 million people that stretched from present-day Ecuador to Chile. As the Inca Empire grew, skilled engineers and architects built as many as 14,000 miles (22,531 km) of stone roads, known as the Inca Trail. Hundreds of white granite buildings also were built. Machu Picchu was likely built during this time.

No single architect or construction engineer is known to have built Machu Picchu. However, Pachacuti may have ordered it to be built as a way of celebrating the defeat of the Inca's enemies, the Chancas.

NOTABLE INCAN STRUCTURES

The Inca Trail
The Inca Trail is a 14,291-mile (23,000-km) system of trails that covers much of South America. Started under the reign of Tahuantinsuyo, the trails were initially built for military purposes. However, the best-known part of the trail—the route to Machu Picchu—was a royal road. It was used only for religious and ceremonial purposes.

The Temple of the Sun
The Temple of the Sun, or Koricancha, is located in the ancient capital of Cuzco. The temple was built around 1200 AD. Pachacuti added to the temple during his reign. It was known for its gold and silver decorations and many statues. When the Spanish invaded Cuzco, they built a Christian church over the Inca temple. Today, the building shows a mix of Spanish and Inca culture.

Ruins of the Sun Temple can still be seen at Machu Picchu.

Pachacuti likely consulted with priests and astronomers to plan the orientation of the city. Most buildings are one story high and rectangular in shape. The Inca used materials they found at the site to construct the buildings.

In many places, especially observatories, windows are a **trapezoidal** shape. They slant inward from bottom to top. This helped steady the structures against earthquakes, and it also may have helped the Inca note the movement of the Sun, the Moon, and the constellations in the night sky. In the southern hemisphere, June 21 is midwinter, and December 21 is midsummer. These were important dates for the Inca. Along with equinoxes, the Inca observed the solstices to determine planting and harvesting times.

The Sun, which the Inca called Inti, was believed to be the giver of life and was the focus of celebrations and festivals throughout the year. Pachacuti believed that as the ruler, he was the Sun's son. He built the Temple of the Sun in Cuzco to use as a solar observatory. A similar structure was built in Machu Picchu.

Pisac
Once a fortress, Pisac was built to ward off attacks from neighboring groups. The fortress was built up a hill. At the bottom of the hill, outside the fortress walls, was a small group of stone buildings that served as guardhouses. The actual fortress was farther up the hill. Inside its walls was a small town consisting of several temples and houses.

Ollantaytambo
Ollantaytambo, at the north end of the 26-mile (42-km) Sacred Valley of the Inca, is the site of the ruins of huge rock walls and many shrines and temples. Huge stones lie about, never set in place. According to a legend, people carved the face of the Inca god, Wiracocha, into the mountainside across from Ollantaytambo.

The Science Behind the Building

Builders must plan how a structure will look before workers can begin the construction process. The people who built Machu Picchu adapted the forms of their structures to the conditions of the landscape as much as possible. They set houses with stepped paths on hillsides and built terraces or used flatter areas of ground for agriculture. Using their knowledge of scientific principles, the Inca created buildings and other structures that were both useful and pleasing to look at.

Properties of Stone

Natural materials, such as stone, have always been used for building. Stone is long-lasting, and able to withstand fire and freezing without changing its form. Machu Picchu was built from a type of stone called granite. Granite is one of the hardest rocks known. It also is one of the most durable rocks. For this reason, Machu Picchu's walls have stood up for centuries in almost constantly humid weather. Stone was the perfect construction material for the mountaintop location in a rain forest region subject to heavy rain, fog, and winds.

Some of Machu Picchu's stone steps were made from single pieces of granite. This helped to create a solid and stable path.

Weight

The granite rock used to build Machu Picchu is very heavy. Such a heavy material needs a solid foundation beneath it for stable construction. The site at the top of the ridge had to be leveled and prepared. The Inca used gravel and stone to support the weight of the walls, buildings, and terraces. This careful engineering has prevented the city from shifting due to heavy rain or the weight of so many huge stones. Machu Picchu's granite walls remain largely intact. The terraced fields built on the steep hillsides are still level enough to be farmed today.

Geometry and Angles

The rocks used to build Machu Picchu came in different shapes and sizes. It was the job of the builders to shape the rocks so that they would fit together. Instead of creating blocks, the builders refined the original shape of the rock by cutting and smoothing it into straight lines. They then worked to match up these **polygons** of rock. Finding rocks that fit tightly together was key to the structure's success. To make a strong structure, the rocks had to be matched up so that no spaces were left between them. The Inca did not use any form of **mortar** or cement to hold the rocks in place. The goal was to have the differently shaped rocks link together like a jigsaw puzzle so that they would stay together.

Science and Technology

Machu Picchu's impressive stone structures were built by hand. The Inca understood the science of their natural world and of construction. They used this knowledge, as well as physical labor, to cut, shape, and move the heavy stones.

Cutting the Rock

Machu Picchu was constructed of white granite taken from an on-site quarry. Without the aid of power tools to cut the stones from the quarry, Inca workers relied on the natural features of the rock to help them instead. They may have used the principle of the wedge to split larger pieces into those of a more manageable size. A wedge is a simple pointed tool used to separate two objects when force is applied. Such a tool might have been made from bronze, the hardest metal that was available to the Inca. The wedge would have been hammered into cracks in the rock, forcing it to break apart.

A chisel is a type of wedge that can be used, along with a mallet, to shape rock.

Moving the Rock

Although the granite was located at the building site, its heavy weight would have made it difficult to move into place. The process of construction at Machu Picchu is not known, but it is possible that Inca workers used a method similar to other projects of the time. Near Lake Titicaca, south of Cuzco, stones for another city's construction were dragged by laborers, using ropes made of vines and hemp. Evidence of drag marks was found on many stones. Given the size of some granite blocks at Machu Picchu, it would have taken many laborers and a great deal of time to move them even a short distance. This may be why it took 10 years to build the city.

The granite blocks were different sizes and shapes, some with as many as 32 corners.

Ramps are often used to move heavy objects from one place to the next.

Ramps

The Inca may have used a ramp, or inclined plane, to move heavy objects. The inclined plane is a flat surface that has been placed on an angle so that its ends are at different heights. It takes less force to push, slide, or drag an object up the angled ramp than to lift the object straight up to a higher level. The Inca may have placed a flat stone on a slope and used it as a ramp on which to drag other stones to the proper location. To move stones from a higher to a lower location, the Inca would have used the force of gravity.

Levers

A number of the houses at Machu Picchu were built two stories high. Some of the stone blocks used to build them are the height of a person. To lift these massive rocks into place, the Inca may have used the lever, a simple machine that can help to lift a load. A lever can be balanced on a central point called a fulcrum to make the load seem lighter to lift—much like a seesaw. If one end of the lever is pushed down, the other end will rise. The Inca may have built levers of the same stone as the blocks so they would be strong enough to lift the weight.

Quick Bites

- Some of the blocks of granite used to construct Machu Picchu weigh more than 50 tons (45 tonnes).
- The Inca's method of counting, called *quipus*, was a series of knots in colored strings. This may be how they kept track of materials, costs, and time.

Computer-Aided Design

Architects are trained professionals who work with clients to design structures. Before anything is built, they make detailed drawings or models. These plans are important tools that help people visualize what the structure will look like. A blueprint is a detailed diagram that shows where all the parts of the structure will be placed. Walls, doors, windows, plumbing, electrical wiring, and other details are mapped out on the blueprint. Blueprints act as a guide for engineers and builders during construction.

For centuries, architects and builders worked without the aid of computers. Sketches and blueprints were drawn by hand. Highly skilled drafters would draw very technical designs. Today, this process is done using computers and sophisticated software programs. Architects use CAD, or computer-aided design, throughout the design process. Early CAD systems used computers to draft building plans. Today's computer programs can do much more. They can build three-dimensional models and computer simulations of how a building will look. They can also calculate the effects of different physical forces on the structure. Using CAD, today's architects can build more complex structures at lower cost and in less time.

Computer-aided design programs have been used since the 1960s.

Eye on Design

Machu Picchu Virtual Tour

To take an online tour of the ruins, type "Machu Picchu virtual tour" in any search engine.

Hundreds of thousands of people visit Machu Picchu each year. However, many people are not able to visit Peru to see this amazing structure. Staff and students from California State University developed a virtual tour that brings Machu Picchu to life in other parts of the world. Team members took several trips to Machu Picchu to snap a collection of more than 5,000 images. Using computers, they fit the images together to create **panoramas**. They added sounds they had recorded at the site. Users simply click the location on a map of Machu Picchu to take a "tour" of a specific part of the ancient city.

The tour made its debut in 2003 at the Hayward Campus Museum during an exhibit called "In the Shadow of Machu Picchu: Andean Life, Past and Present." Yale University's Peabody Museum of Natural History took the tour on the road the following year as part of a traveling exhibition called "Unveiling the Mystery of the Incas."

Since then, a number of virtual tours of Machu Picchu have been developed. These tours take people on a journey back in time to a place they may not otherwise have the chance to experience.

Location

Machu Picchu is located on a ridge in the Andes Mountains of Peru, 43 miles (70 km) northwest of Cuzco. The ridge overlooks the winding Urubamba River gorge and lies between two mountains—Machu Picchu, or "Old Peak," and Huayna Picchu, or "New Peak."

Elevation

The ancient city was built 7,710 feet (2,350 m) above sea level.

Area

- The buildings and terraced farmland of Machu Picchu cover an area of 5 square miles (13 sq km).

Other Interesting Facts

- The temperature in and around Machu Picchu remains close to 60° Fahrenheit (16° Celsius) year-round.
- In all, about 100 stairways, containing 3,000 steps, connect parts of Machu Picchu.

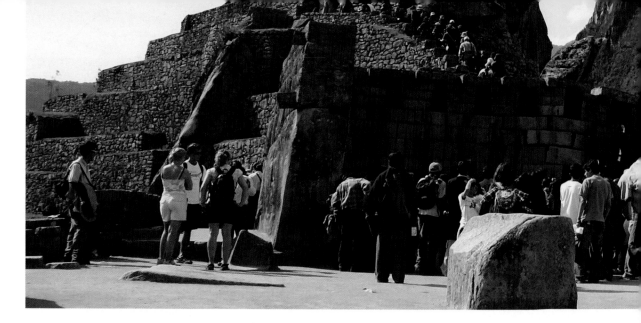

Environmental Viewpoint

For almost four centuries after it was abandoned by the Inca, nature took over as the caretaker of Machu Picchu, all but hiding it from human view. When Hiram Bingham located it in 1911, a few local farmers were using parts of the terraced fields to grow beans and corn. The walls, stairways, and buildings lay beneath thick forest vines, underbrush, and moss. They were protected from the rain forest climate. Shrouded in fog and drenched in heavy rain, the stonework of the city remained intact. Only the thatched roofs of the buildings gave in to the elements in the natural process of **decomposition**.

Since that time, Machu Picchu has become a well-known tourist site. In one year, the ruins can host up to 400,000 people from around the world. This number of people can have a powerful impact on the site and its surroundings. Already, there is fear that the stonework is being harmed from handling by the large number of people who explore the site. Pollution is also becoming a concern. Many people do not take their trash with them when they leave the site.

To handle the increase in tourists, plans are being made to build a cable-car track to the site. If this plan moves forward, parts of the rain forest will be cut down to build the tracks. This will further harm the fragile **ecosystem**. As well, more tourists will be able to visit Machu Picchu, potentially causing more damage to the site.

As many as 2,000 people visit parts of Machu Picchu each day. Walking on the ruins is causing them to erode.

INDING SOLUTIONS

In 1983, Machu Picchu was declared a UNESCO World Heritage Site. The hope was that this would help protect the site from further harm. Instead, the United Nations has stated that Machu Picchu is one of the most endangered heritage sites in the world.

The Peruvian government is working toward preserving Machu Picchu and its surrounding area. Plans are in place to reduce the number of people visiting the site—especially those hiking to it via the Inca Trail. Today, anyone hiking to Machu Picchu must be registered with the government and must travel with an official tour guide. The guide is to make sure that hikers stay on the trail and dispose of their waste properly. Hiking groups cannot be larger than 40 people, including the guide, cook, porters, and crew. On any given day, only 500 people, including crews, are allowed to begin the hike. This is down from the more than 1,000 people that used to leave daily. Once tourists reach Machu Picchu, groups can stay for no more than four days.

Construction Careers

Stonemasons, stone carvers, metalworkers, laborers, roof thatchers, and farmers were among the people who worked on the construction of Machu Picchu. People from many job fields helped build the site, since each person in the empire paid his or her taxes to the ruler in the form of work.

Stonemasons

The Inca used of a method of **dry stone construction** to build walls, structures, steps, and terraces. As part of this process, stonemasons took blocks of granite from a quarry within Machu Picchu. The blocks were then cut using stone and bronze tools. They were polished using sand or other stones to create flat surfaces. The finished blocks, called ashlar, were fitted together so tightly that they did not need mortar to hold them in place. This method creates a wall stable enough to withstand earthquake motion. The craft of stonemasonry is still used worldwide to create buildings, structures, and sculptures.

Laborers

Laborers were responsible for doing many tasks during the construction of Machu Picchu. They helped to level the ground before buildings were constructed. They also moved granite blocks from the quarry to each building site and helped to lift them into place. Some laborers constructed the stepped terraces where the city's food supply was grown. Others built the water irrigation system. Laborers likely planted the first crops of corn and beans. Laborers still play an important role on job sites. They clean sites, operate equipment, and load materials, among other things. Some labor jobs require experience. Others can be done without special training.

Roof Thatcher

The buildings of Machu Picchu mainly were made of stone. The roofs, however, were **thatched**. Making a thatched roof requires skilled workers. They must understand the materials and processes involved in using plants to make a roof that does not leak. To make the roofs at Machu Picchu, the thatchers chose a coarse bunch grass called *ichu*. The thatchers would tie the ichu into bundles and fasten them to the roof beams. They placed many layers of bundles down the roof. The end thatches were tied to pegs that stuck out from the roof. This kept them from being blown away. When done properly, the roof would protect the inside of the building for 10 to 15 years. At that time, the thatching would be redone. Today, roofs in places near Machu Picchu, such as Cuzco, often are made from tiles.

Notable Structures

The Inca were just one group of people to realize the durability of stone. People from different parts of the world have been using stone to construct buildings for thousands of years. Many of these structures still exist today—some in their entirety and others in part.

Great Pyramid

Built: 2600–2480 BC

Location: El Giza, Egypt

Design: King Khufu

Description: The Great Pyramid is one of the three pyramids at Giza. This structure was built of cut stone blocks. The pyramid is thought to have about 2,300,000 blocks in total, more than any other structure ever built.

Tikal

Built: 800–200 BC

Location: Guatemala

Design: Yax Ehb' Xook

Description: Tikal was a major site of **Mayan** civilization. This site is built of cut stone and has thousands of structures, including public plazas that are accessed by ramps and five temples. Much of the site is still buried by mounds of earth and forest plants. It was occupied from the 6th century BC to the 10th century AD.

The lasting quality of stone construction has ensured that something of these ancient structures remain for people today to learn about life in the past.

Angkor Wat

Built: 1140 AD

Location: Cambodia, Southeast Asia

Design: King Suryavarman II

Description: This Hindu temple, built of stone masonry, was originally enclosed by a moat and wall. A 213-foot (65-m) tower in the center was built without mortar, similar to walls in Machu Picchu. Abandoned in 1431, Angkor Wat is one of the world's largest religious structures.

Mont St. Michel

Built: 1203 and later

Location: Mont St. Michel, France

Design: William de Volpiano

Description: This monastery built of cut stone sits on an island in Normandy. It was once connected to mainland France by a land bridge that was submerged at high tide. The bridge later became a **causeway**. Mont St. Michel was named by UNESCO as a World Heritage Site in 1979.

Stone Structures Around the World

Stone structures are found in countries around the world. Some were built centuries ago by ancient civilizations, using very basic tools.

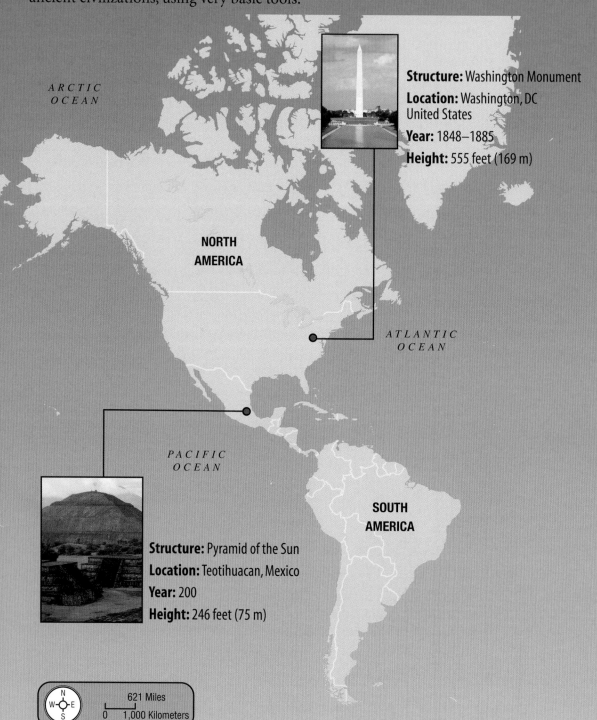

Structure: Washington Monument
Location: Washington, DC United States
Year: 1848–1885
Height: 555 feet (169 m)

ARCTIC OCEAN

NORTH AMERICA

ATLANTIC OCEAN

PACIFIC OCEAN

SOUTH AMERICA

Structure: Pyramid of the Sun
Location: Teotihuacan, Mexico
Year: 200
Height: 246 feet (75 m)

621 Miles
0   1,000 Kilometers

Others have been built in more recent times, by people who have access to modern technologies. This map outlines some of the world's best-known stone structures.

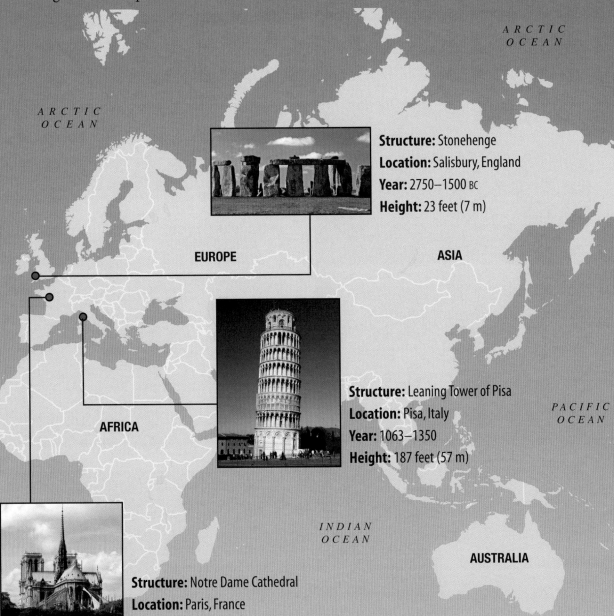

ARCTIC OCEAN

ARCTIC OCEAN

EUROPE

ASIA

Structure: Stonehenge
Location: Salisbury, England
Year: 2750–1500 BC
Height: 23 feet (7 m)

Structure: Leaning Tower of Pisa
Location: Pisa, Italy
Year: 1063–1350
Height: 187 feet (57 m)

PACIFIC OCEAN

AFRICA

INDIAN OCEAN

AUSTRALIA

Structure: Notre Dame Cathedral
Location: Paris, France
Year: 1163–1250
Height: 110 feet (34 m)

Quiz

Q Why was Machu Picchu so hard to find?

A It was hidden on a mountaintop ridge deep in the forest and was overgrown with plant life.

Q What special construction style did the ancient Inca use to build walls in Machu Picchu?

A They used dry stone construction with granite blocks.

Q Why did the Inca build terraced agricultural fields?

A It was not possible to grow crops on the steep slopes of mountains in Peru.

Q What is the Intihuatana Stone?

A It is a pillar of rock that acts like a sundial to show the spring and fall equinox.

Make a Star Clock

The Inca used the Sun, Moon, and stars as a calendar. Try making this star clock to help you find out the date and time.

Materials
- pencil
- paper
- bristleboard or other cardboard
- wristwatch

Instructions

1. On a piece of paper, draw two circles like the ones on this page. Copy the pictures and words onto the two circles, and cut the circles from the paper.

2. Paste each circle on the cardboard.

3. Place the small circle on top of the large circle. Push a pencil through the center of both circles to hold them together.

4. On a clear night, go outside. Find the North Star, as shown on the face of your star clock. Face the North Star.

5. Find the current month around the outside circle of the star clock. Put your thumb over the current month. Hold the star clock so your thumb is at the top.

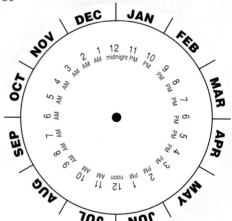

6. Turn the smaller circle until its stars look the same as those in the sky.

7. Read the time in the window. If you are on Daylight Savings Time, add one hour. How does the star clock's time compare to the time on the wristwatch?

Further Research

You can find out more about the Inca and Machu Picchu at your local library or on the Internet.

Websites

For more information on Machu Picchu, visit
http://wmf.org/watch2008/watch.php?id=S407

To learn more about the ancient Inca culture, check out
www.nationalgeographic.com/inca

Find out about Peru at
www.peru.info/perueng.asp

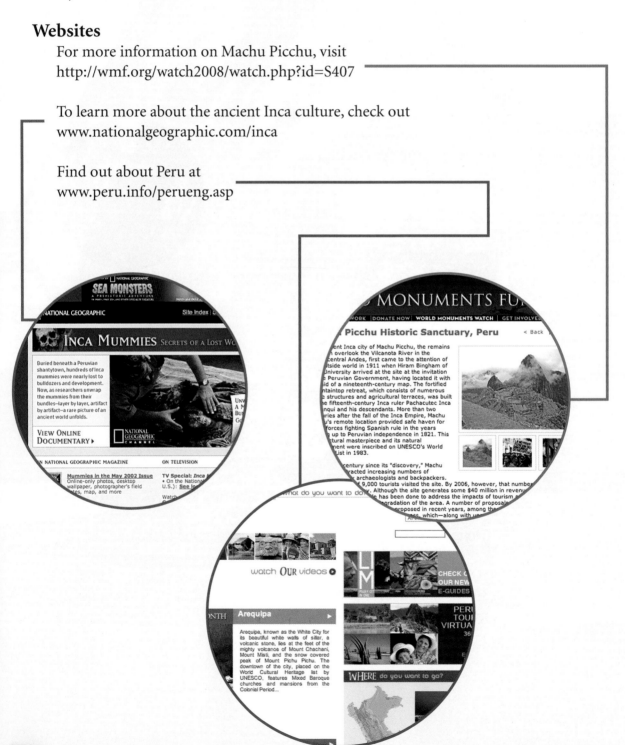

Glossary

archaeological: relating to studying about the past by digging up and examining old structures and objects

causeway: a raised path or road that crosses water

decomposition: the process of breaking down something into smaller parts

dry stone construction: made without mortar

ecosystem: a community of living things and the place where they live

equinox: the time when there are equal hours of daylight and darkness

gravity: the force that attracts objects toward the center of Earth

irrigated: applied water in dry areas to assist in growing crops

mausoleum: a building that houses a tomb

Mayan: an American Indian of Mexico and Central America

mortar: a building material like cement that hardens to hold objects together

observatory: a building used to study the sky

panoramas: continuous views of a certain place

polygons: geometric shapes that have many sides

retreat: a place for religious contemplation

sentinel: a soldier or guard that keeps watch

solstice: the time when the Sun is farthest from the equator

sundial: a device that measures time by showing the position of the Sun

terraced: set on a series of level platforms that are built on a steep slope to create farmland on otherwise unusable terrain

thatched: covered with a natural vegetation like straw or reeds

trapezoidal: a four-sided shape with two parallel and two uneven sides

UNESCO World Heritage Site: a site designated by the United Nations to be of great cultural worth to the world and in need of protection

Index